Reader Rabbit® STICKERS

Completion Sticker

When you have completed this book, go to www.thelearningcompany.com/workbooks to download and print your Personalized Achievement Certificate. Once printed, place this sticker on your certificate and display proudly.

© 2011 by HMH Consumer Company. All rights reserved. www.thelearningcompany.com

Seaside Delight

Reader and Sam are enjoying the sun and surf at the beach. Join in their fun, and you will learn about counting and writing numbers!

You will have fun with the following activities:
- Writing numbers and counting
- Matching number words to numbers
- Drawing objects to match a number

Let's have some fun!

Note to Parents, Teachers, and Caregivers:
Read the directions aloud to your children. Help children complete the activities. Offer guidance, encouragement, and praise to instill a love of learning.

Visit www.thelearningcompany.com/workbooks for FREE learning games!

Writing Numbers

Trace each number.

How many objects do you count? Write each number.

Writing Numbers

Trace each number.

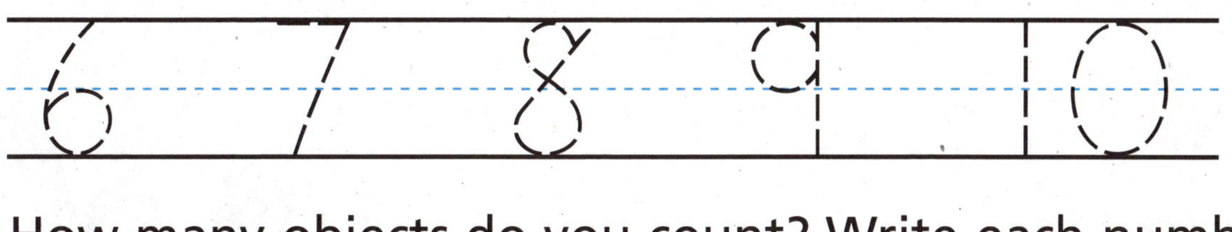

How many objects do you count? Write each number.

Writing Numbers

Write the number of suns in the square next to them.

Writing Numbers

Trace each number.

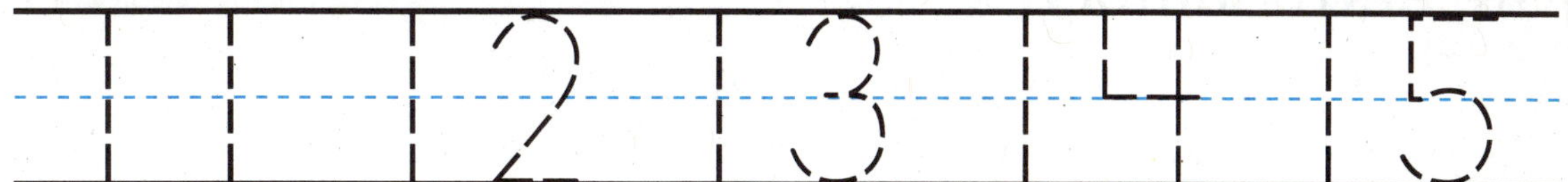

How many objects do you count? Write each number.

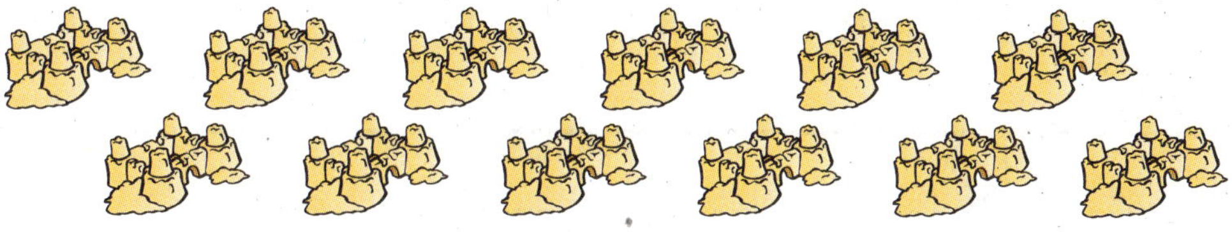

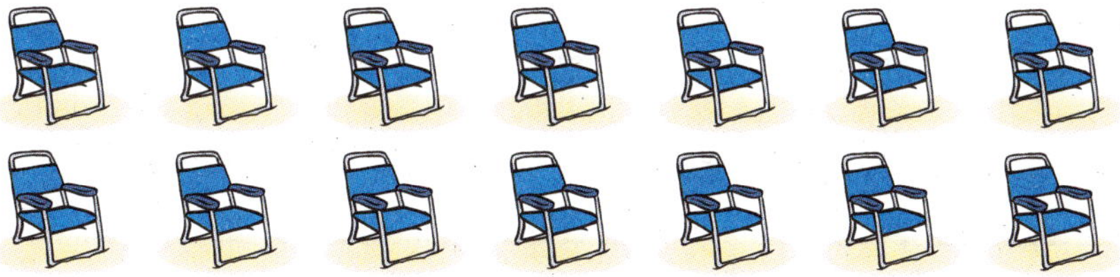

Writing Numbers

Trace each number.
Then write each number.

Counting from 1 to 20

Connect the dots. Start at 1.

Figuring Things Out

How many birds did Reader see?
Write the missing numbers.

Reader saw 🐦🐦🐦🐦 .
Then he saw 🐦🐦 .

Step 1: Count. 🐦🐦🐦🐦 _____

Step 2: Count on. 🐦🐦 _____

_____

Reader saw _____ birds in all.

Writing Missing Numbers

Write the missing numbers.

Matching Words to Numbers

Trace each word. Then write each number.
The first one has been done for you.

Matching Words to Numbers

Trace each word. Then write each number.
The first one has been done for you.

Matching Words to Numbers

Match each word to its number. Draw a line from the
sand castle to the pail with the same number.
The first one has been done for you.

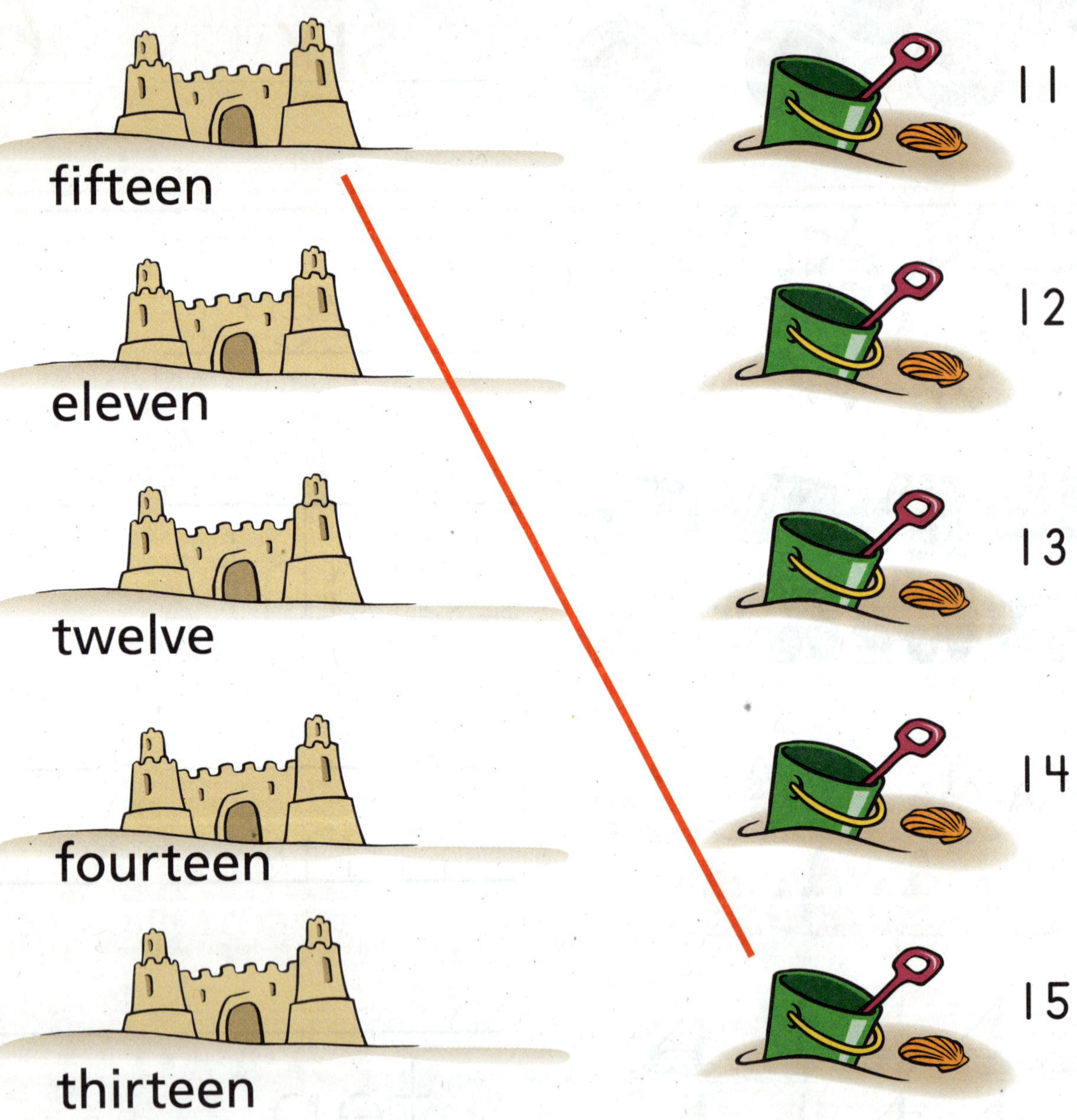

Matching Words to Numbers

Write the numbers that show the score of each
volleyball game.

twenty   sixteen

eighteen   seventeen

twelve   nineteen

eleven   thirteen

Matching Numbers to Objects

Color each group to match the number that tells how many objects are in that group. The first one has been done for you.

1 2 3 4 5 6 7 8 9 10

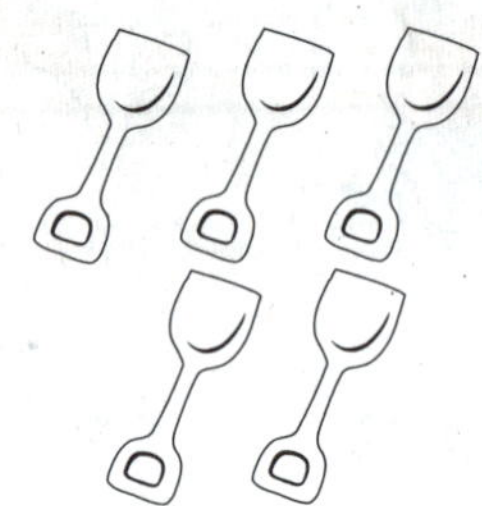

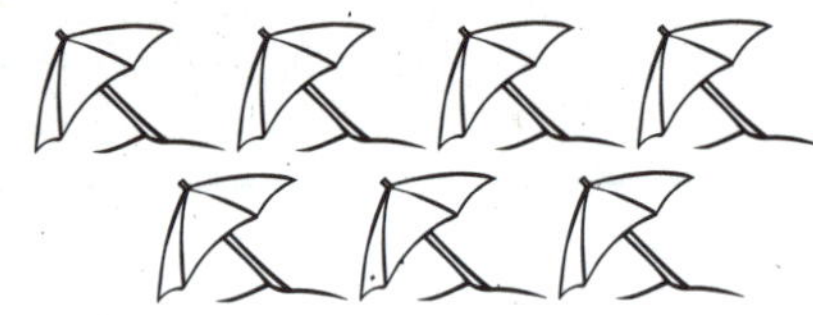

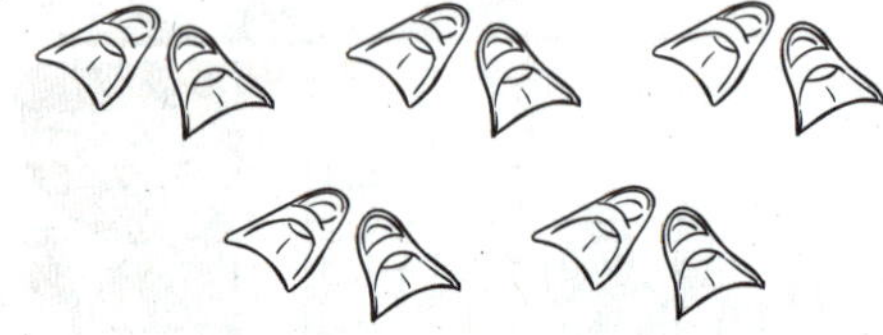

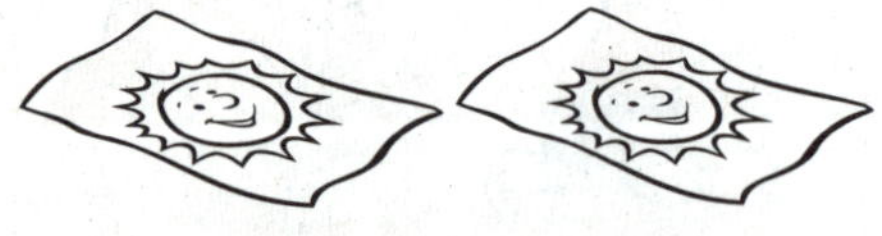

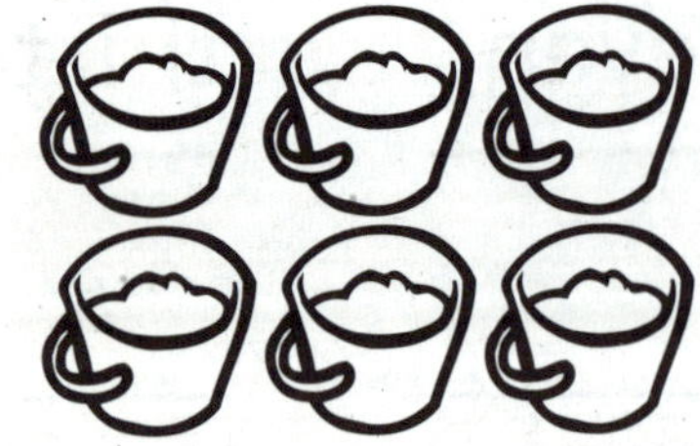

Matching Numbers to Groups of Objects

Draw a line from each group to the number that tells how many objects are in that group.

12

5

8

10

Finding the Group with More

How many objects are in each group? Write the number in the blank. Then circle the group that has **more** objects. The first one has been done for you.

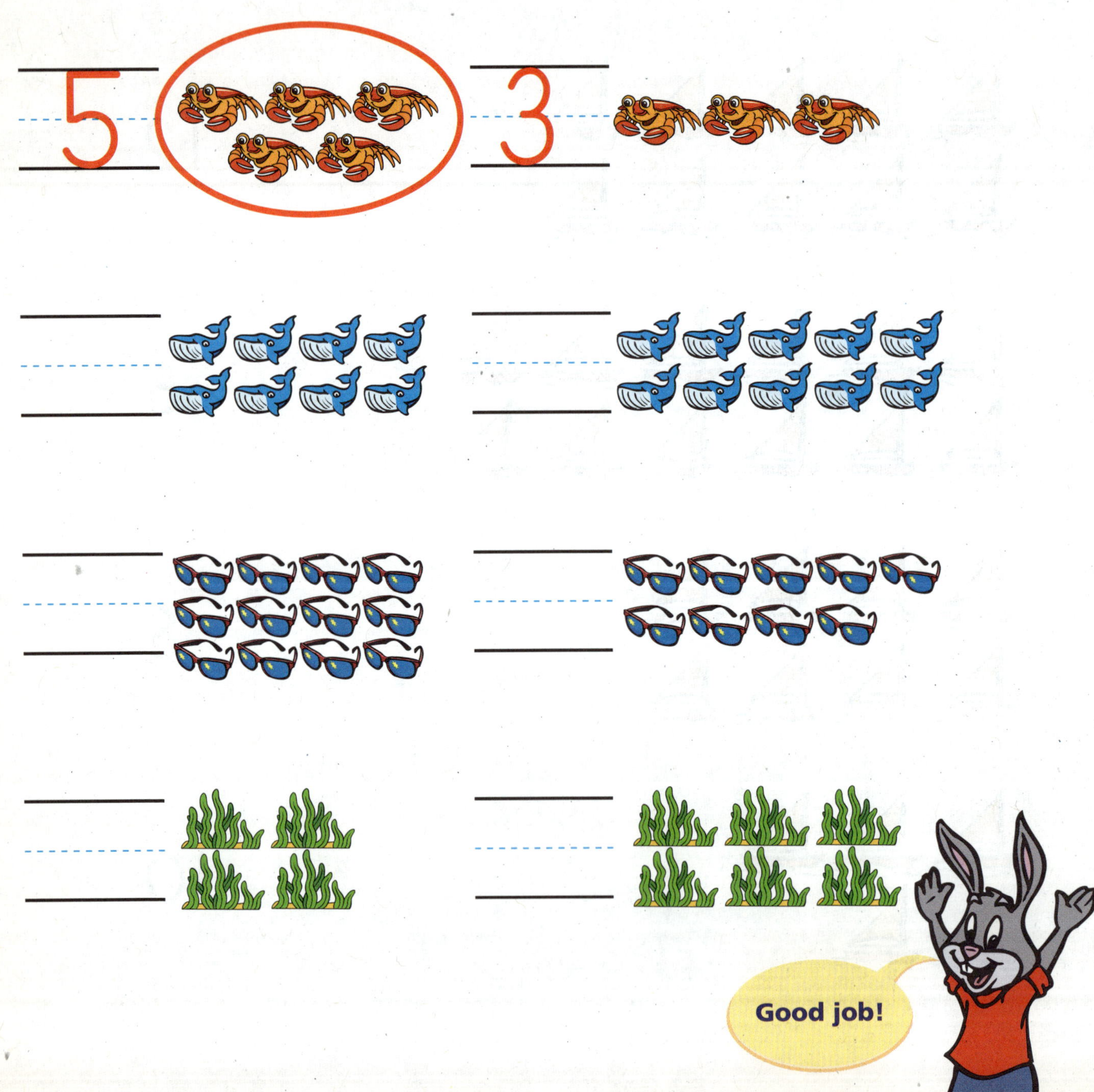

Finding the Group with Fewer

How many objects are in each group? Write the number in the blank. Then circle the group that has **fewer** objects. The first one has been done for you.

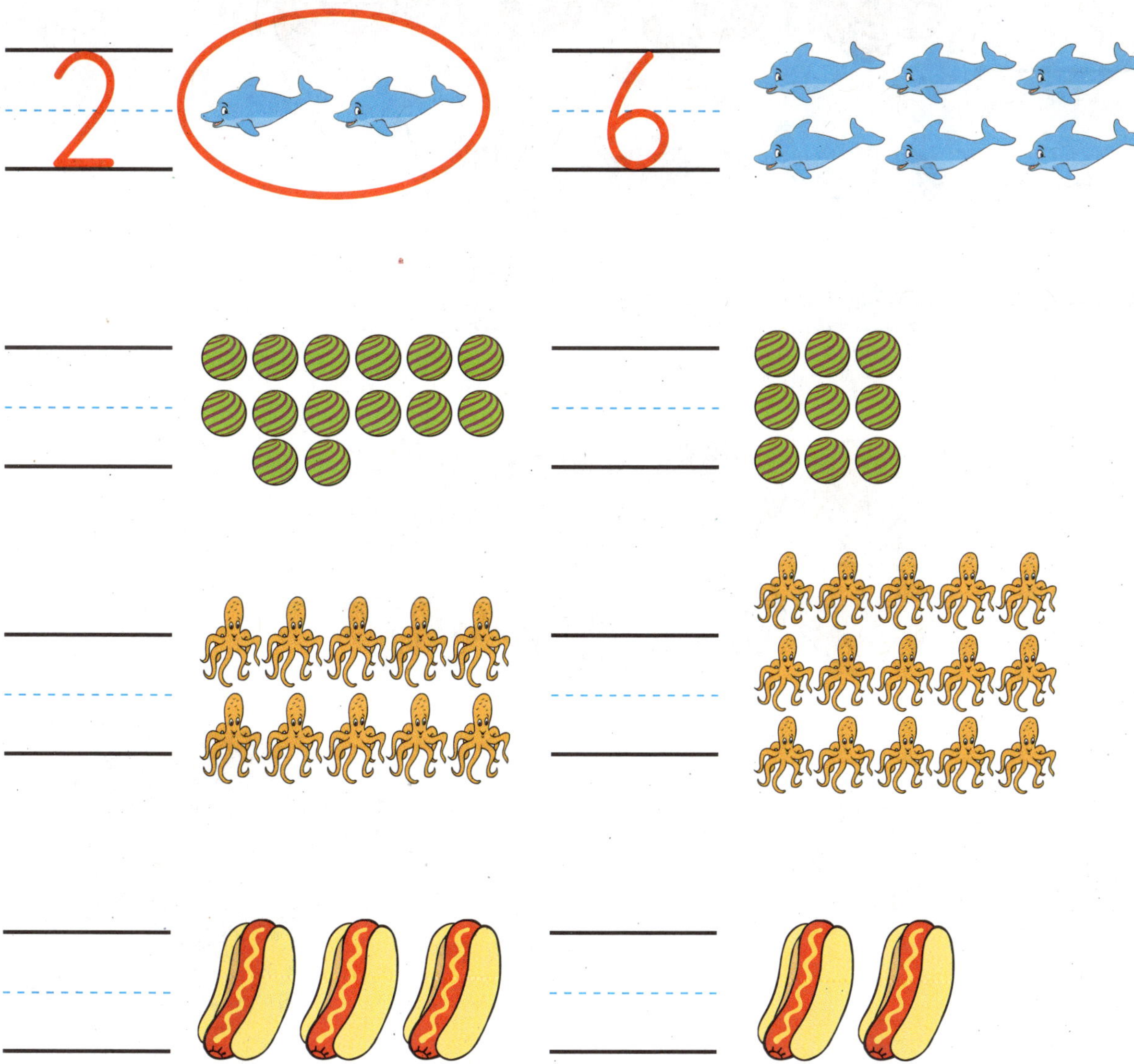

Counting Objects in a Group

Count the objects. Then write the number.

Counting Objects in a Group

Count the objects. Then write the number.

Counting Objects in a Group

Count the number of beach balls, towels, and dolphins. Then color the objects in each group to match the color of the number that tells how many objects are in each group.

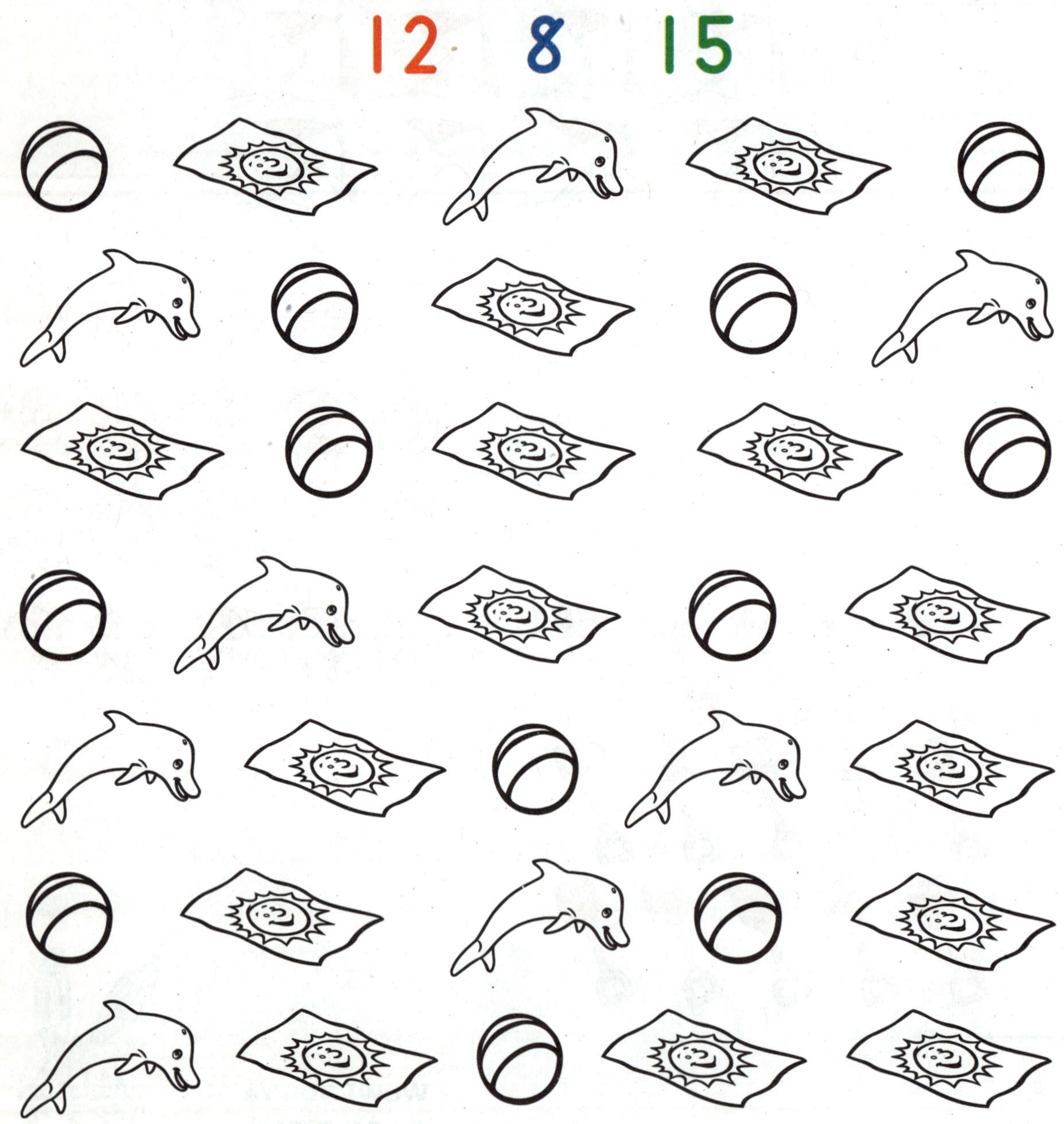

Drawing Objects to Show How Many

Draw the objects to match the number.

3  

4  

5  

6  

Drawing Objects to Show How Many

Draw the objects to match the number.

7 

10 

13 

Drawing Objects to Show How Many

Draw the objects to match the number.

5 

8 

14 

Counting from 1 to 100

On the beach one night, Reader looked up into the sky and saw many stars. Help him count them. Write the missing numbers in the stars.

Writing Numbers

Practice writing the numbers using straight and curved lines. First trace the numbers and then write them.

Numbers with straight lines

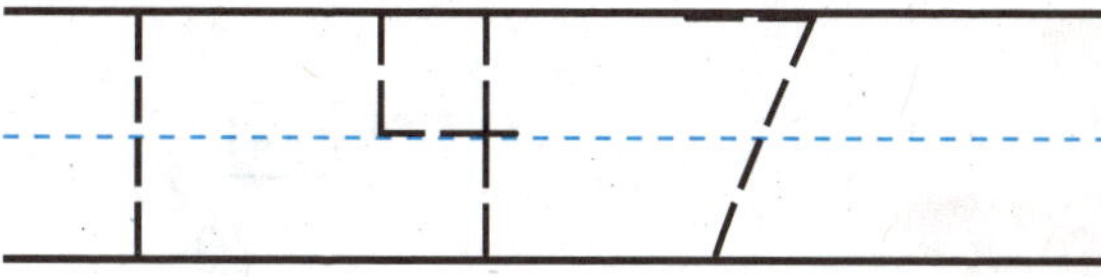

Numbers with curved lines

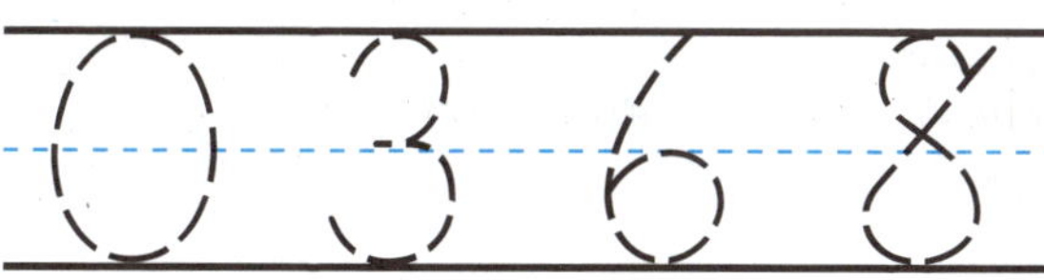

Numbers with both straight and curved lines

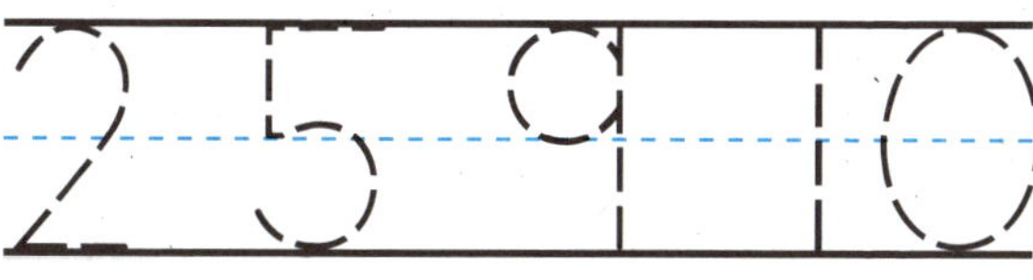

Straight lines look like this:

Curved lines look like this:

**Visit www.thelearningcompany.com/workbooks
for FREE learning games!**

Counting by 2s

Count by 2s. Connect the dots from 2 to 50 in order.

Counting by 5s

Count by 5s to 50. Color only the shells that you count.

5	3	6	4	12
10	15	9	11	22
12	20	14	16	31
14	25	30	41	43
33	32	35	40	47
47	36	43	45	50

Counting by 10s

Reader works at the beach. Every morning he puts flags behind each lifeguard's chair.

Write the numbers on the flags in order beneath the beach chairs. The first one has been done for you.

Counting Backward

Count backward starting at 30. Write each number in the squares and make your way to the seashell. When you get to the end, color the seashell.

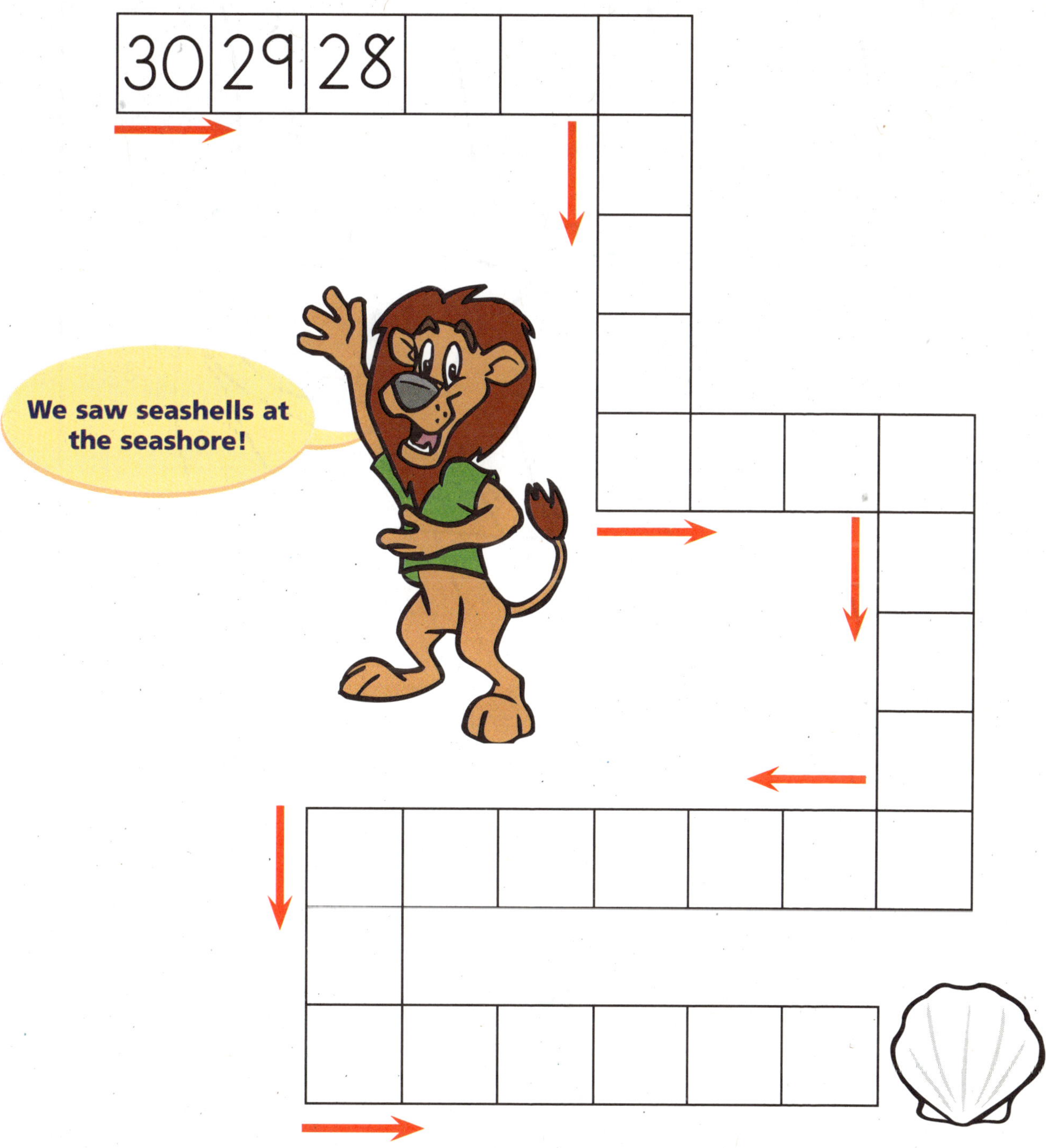

Coloring by Number

Color each section the same color as the matching number below.

Finding the Hidden Numbers

Find the number hidden in each toy chest. Write the number you find on the line beside each chest. The first one has been done for you.

Answer Key

2 Trace the numbers. 2, 5, 4, 1, 0, 3

3 Trace the numbers. 6, 9, 10, 7, 8

4 1, 2, 3, 4, 5, 6, 7, 8, 9, 10

5 Trace the numbers. 13, 12, 11, 14, 15

6 Trace and write each number.

7 Connect the dots to make a whale.

8 4, 2, 6

9 3, 5, 8, 11, 12, 14, 17, 19

10 Trace the words. 2, 3, 4, 5

11 Trace the words. 7, 8, 9, 10

12 eleven to 11, twelve to 12, fourteen to 14, thirteen to 13

13 20, 16; 18, 17; 12, 19; 11, 13

14 pink shovels, brown umbrellas, black flippers, blue beach towels, red beach buckets, green seashells, purple fish, yellow boats, silver beach balls

15 10 boats to 10, 12 boats to 12, 8 boats to 8, 5 boats to 5

16 8, 10, circle group of 10; 12, 9, circle group of 12; 4, 6, circle group of 6

17 14, 9, circle group of 9; 10, 15, circle group of 10; 3, 2, circle group of 2

18 4, 6, 8, 1, 2

19 13, 20, 15

20 12 red beach balls, 8 blue dolphins, 15 green beach towels

21 2 snails, 3 fish, 4 boats, 5 shells

22 6 umbrellas, 9 towels, 12 beach balls

23 4 shovels, 7 buckets, 13 water drops

24 5, 6, 7, 8, 9, 12, 13, 14, 15, 16, 17, 18, 19, 23, 24, 25, 26, 27, 28, 29, 31, 32, 33, 34, 35, 36, 37, 38, 39, 41, 42, 43, 44, 45, 46, 47, 48, 49, 51, 52, 53, 54, 55, 56, 57, 58, 59, 61, 62, 63, 64, 65, 66, 67, 68, 69, 71, 72, 73, 74, 75, 76, 77, 78, 79, 81, 82, 83, 84, 85, 86, 87, 88, 89, 91, 92, 93, 94, 95, 96, 97, 98, 99

25 Trace and write the numbers.

26 Connect the dots to make a fish.

27 5, 10, 15, 20, 25, 30, 35, 40, 45, 50

28 30, 40, 50, 60, 70, 80, 90, 100

29 right arrow: 27, 26, 25

down arrow: 24, 23, 22, 21

right arrow: 20, 19, 18

down arrow: 17, 16, 15, 14

left arrow: 13, 12, 11, 10, 9, 8

down arrow: 7, 6

right arrow: 5, 4, 3, 2, 1

30 Color by number.

31 4, 10, 2, 8, 16

Zippity Zoo

Reader and Sam are having a great time visiting all the animals at the zoo. Come along and learn about shapes.

You will have fun with the following activities:
- Finding shapes
- Sorting shapes
- Comparing shapes

Let's see what is at the zoo!

Learning About Squares

A **square** is a shape that has four sides. All the sides are the same length. Trace the square below and draw a picture inside it.

Finding Squares

A **square** has four sides that are the same length. Color the squares in the tree. Then write how many squares you find.

____

________ squares

Drawing Squares

Trace the **square** around each animal.

Now draw a **square** around each animal.

Learning About Triangles

A **triangle** is a shape that has three sides. The sides can can be the same or different lengths. Trace the triangle below and draw a picture inside it.

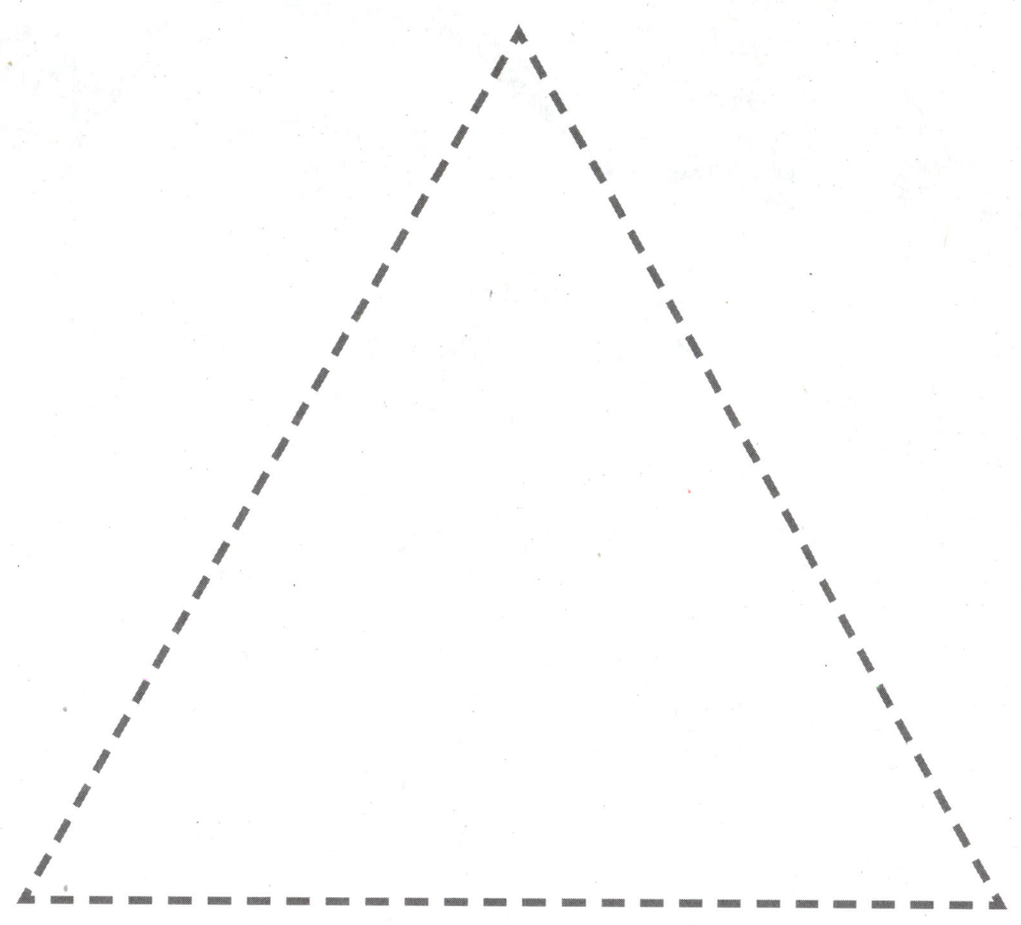

Finding Triangles

Draw a line through the **triangles** Reader passes as he walks through the jungle maze.

Finding Squares and Triangles

Color the **squares** on the turtle's shell **green**. Color the **triangles** on the turtle's shell **red**. Then write how many squares and triangles you find.

______ squares

______ triangles

Learning About Circles

A **circle** is a curved shape that is perfectly round. Trace the circle below and draw a picture inside it.

Finding Circles

Draw an **X** on the **circles** that you find.
Then color the picture.

Drawing Circles

Trace the **circle** in the center of each flower. Color each circle yellow. Color the petals any color you like.

Learning About Rectangles

A **rectangle** is a special kind of four-sided figure that has its opposite sides the same length. Trace the rectangle below and draw a picture inside it.

Finding Rectangles

Color the **rectangles** on the safari van. Then write
how many rectangles you find.

____

_______ rectangles

Drawing Rectangles

Help Sam find his way to Reader by following the signs.
Trace the **rectangles** along the trail.

Finding Circles and Rectangles

Color the **circles** on the snake **purple**.
Color the **rectangles** on the snake **yellow**.
Then write how many circles and
rectangles you find.

__________ circles   __________ rectangles

Learning About Trapezoids

A **trapezoid** has four sides.
Two of the sides are slanted.
Trace the top trapezoid.
Then color the others.

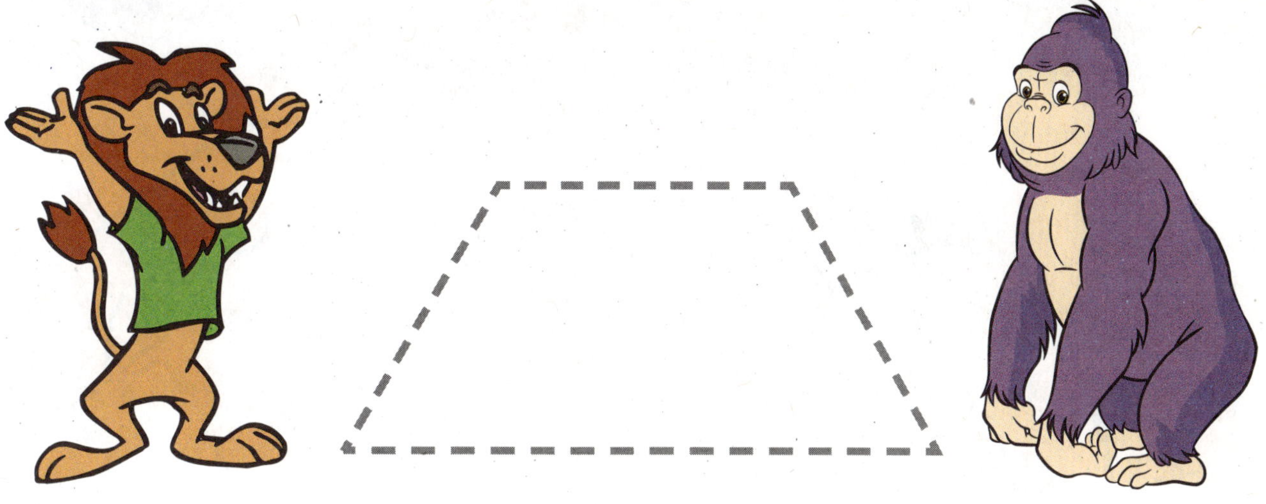

Drawing Trapezoids

Trace the **trapezoids** to help the gorilla find his home. Then color the trapezoid that you think is big enough to be his home.

Learning About Hexagons and Octagons

Hexagons have six sides.
Color the **hexagons** blue.
Octagons have eight sides.
Color the **octagons** red.

STOP

Kangaroo Crossing

Tigers Live Here

No Swimming

Feeding Zone

Monkeys Ahead

No Littering

Quiet, Animals Sleeping

Be Careful

Drawing Hexagons and Octagons

Trace your own signs and color the signs any color you want. Then answer the questions.

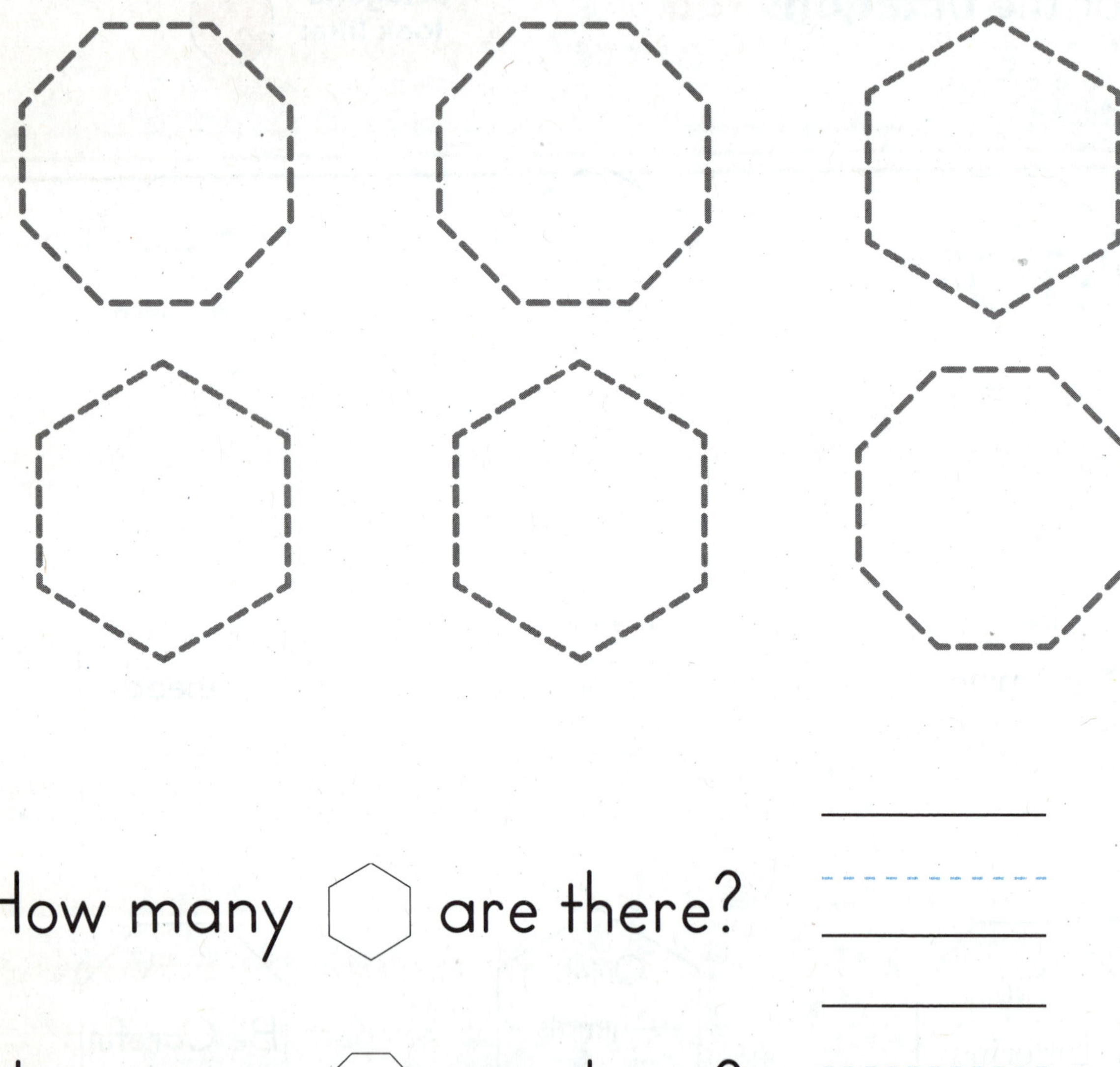

How many ⬡ are there? ______

How many ⯃ are there? ______

Finding Shapes

Circle the 10 shapes that you find in the tree. Then write how many shapes you find.

circles	________
trapezoids	________
triangles	________
rectangles	________
octagons	________
hexagons	________

Finding Shapes

Look at these shapes.

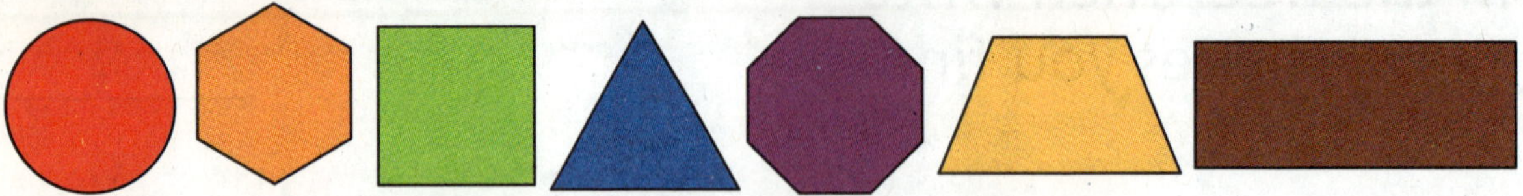

Can you find these shapes in this picture? Color the shapes in the picture the same color as they are above.

Finding Shapes

Reader wants to describe the fun he had in the jungle in one word. Can you figure out what word? Read the name of the shape in each group and then circle the letter next to the shape. The first one has been done for you.

Find the triangle.

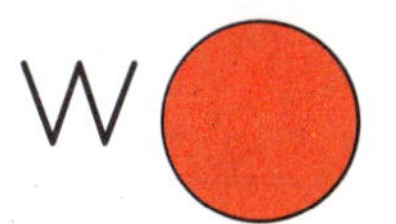

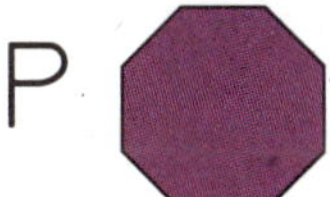

Find the circle.

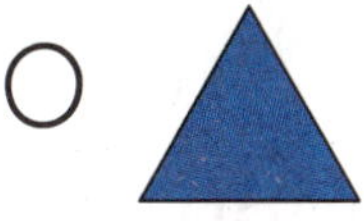
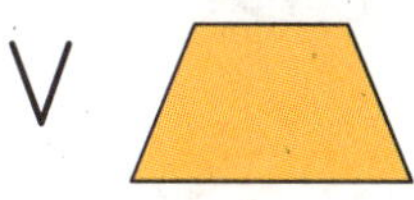

Find the square.

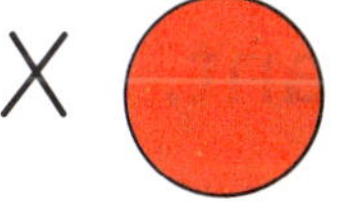

Find the octagon.

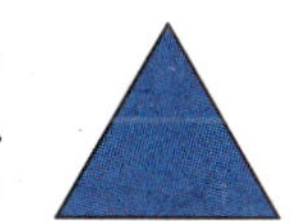

Now write the letters you circled in the blank spaces above the shapes below. Then say the word!

___ ___ ___ T!

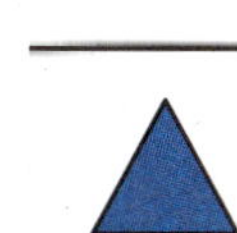
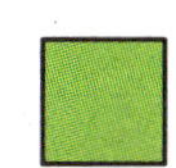
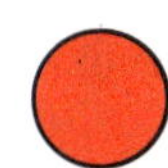
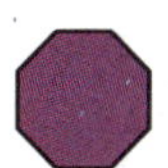

Drawing Shapes

Let's draw some shapes!

Draw a **square** around the elephant.

Draw a **triangle** around the elephant.

Draw a **hexagon** around the elephant.

Draw a **trapezoid** around the elephant.

Finding the Names of Shapes

Draw a line from each shape to its name. The first one has been done for you.

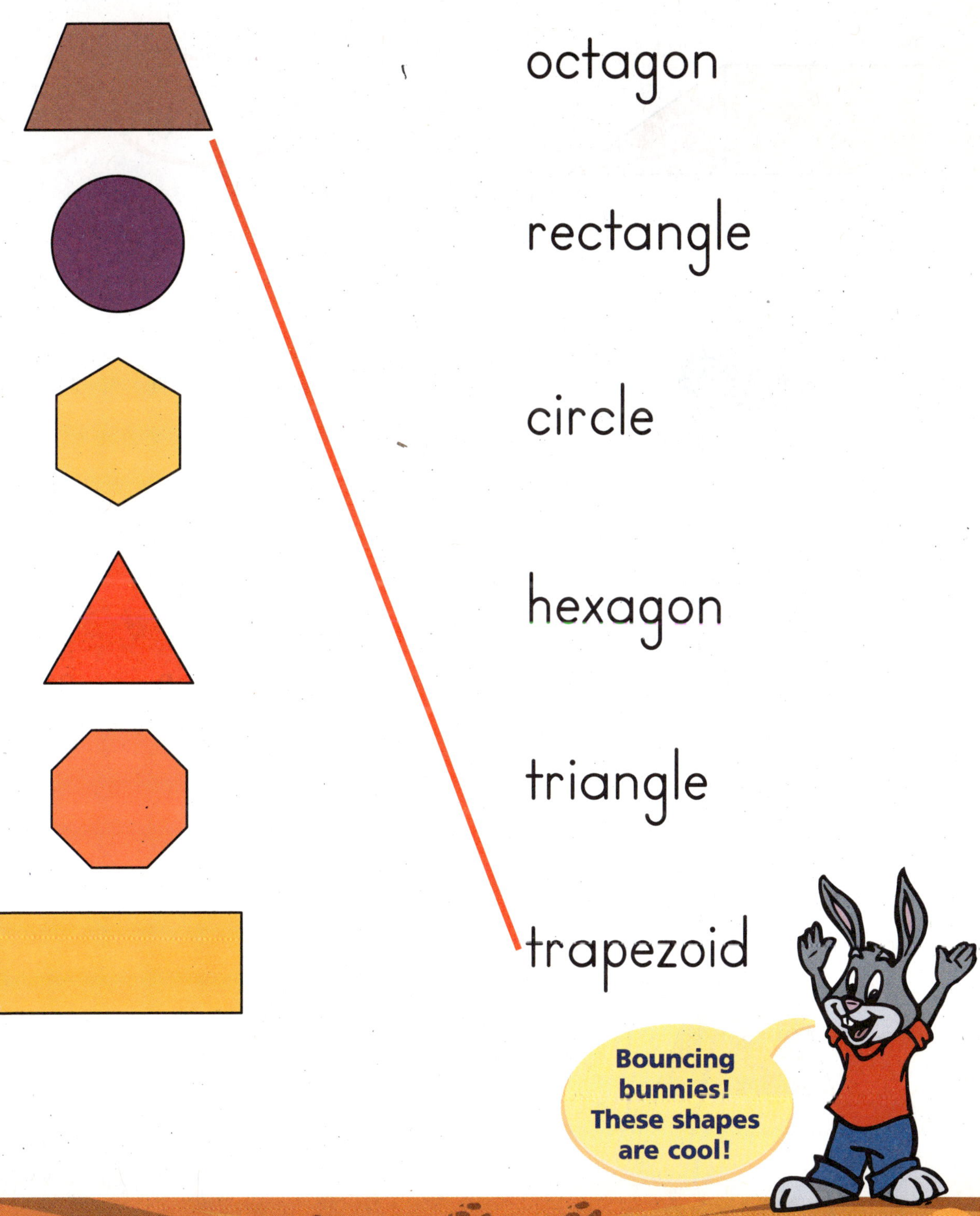

Naming Combined Shapes

Circle the names of the shapes used. The first one has been done for you.

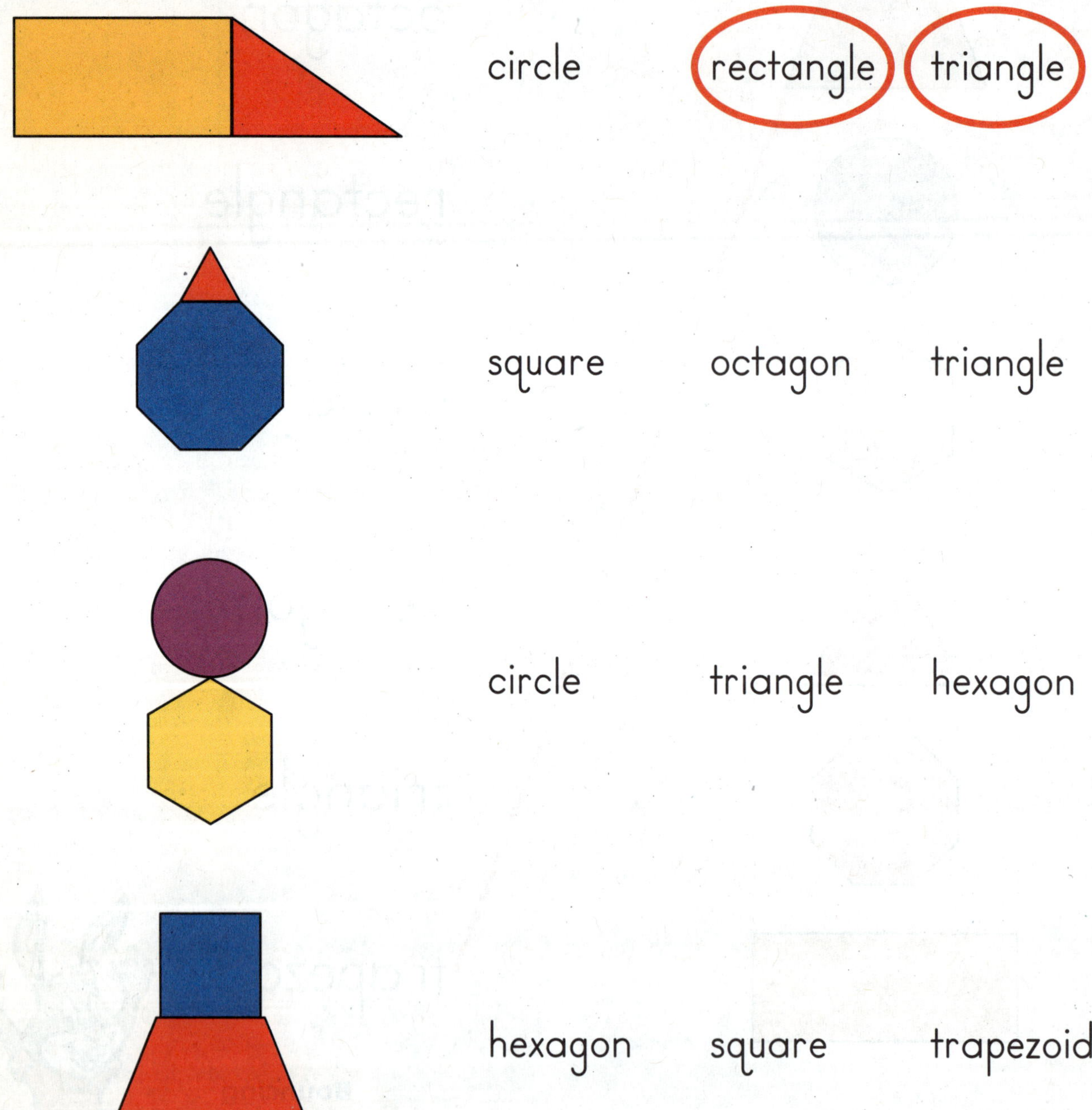

Drawing Combined Shapes

Draw a picture using a  and a 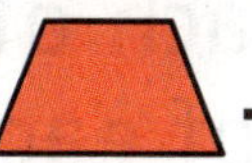 .

Draw a picture using a  and a  .

Writing the Names of Shapes

Trace and color each of the shapes.
Trace the names of each shape.

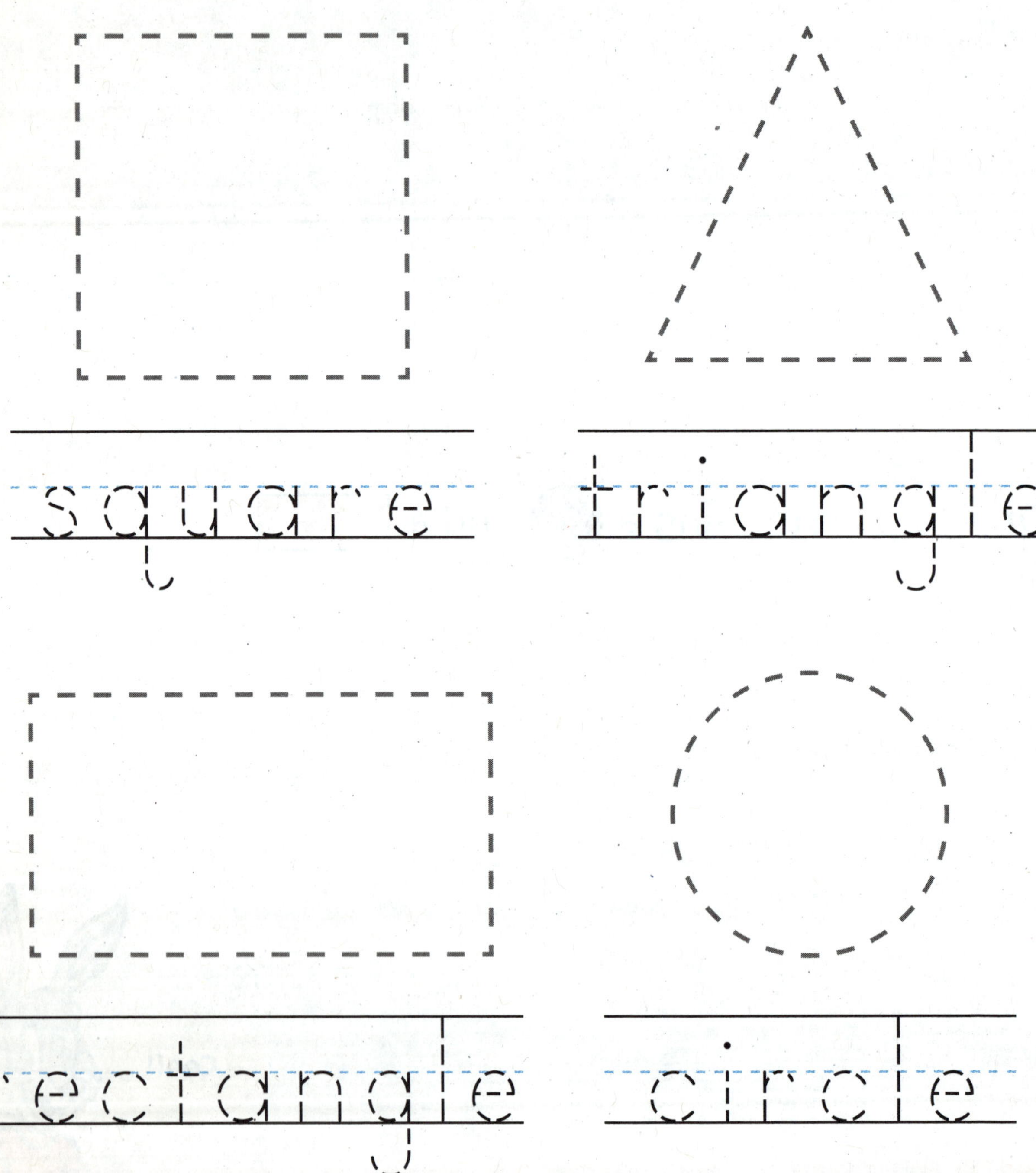

Sorting by Shape

Color all the **squares** blue.

Color all the **triangles** orange.

Color all the **circles** green.

Color all the **trapezoids** red.

Color all the **rectangles** that are not squares purple.

Comparing by Size

Draw an **X** on the square that is **smaller**.

Draw an **X** on the circle that is **bigger**.

Draw an **X** on the trapezoid that is **smaller**.

Draw an **X** on the triangle that is **bigger**.

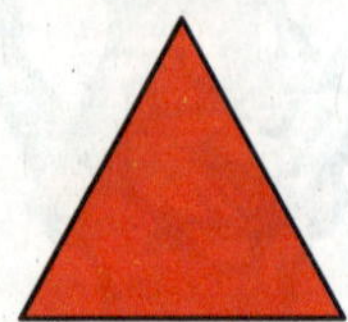

Sorting by Size

Color the **small** shapes **blue**.

Color the **large** shapes **green**.

Matching by Size and Shape

Draw a line between the shapes that are the same size and shape. The first one has been done for you.

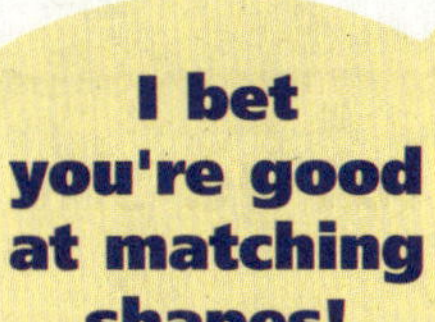

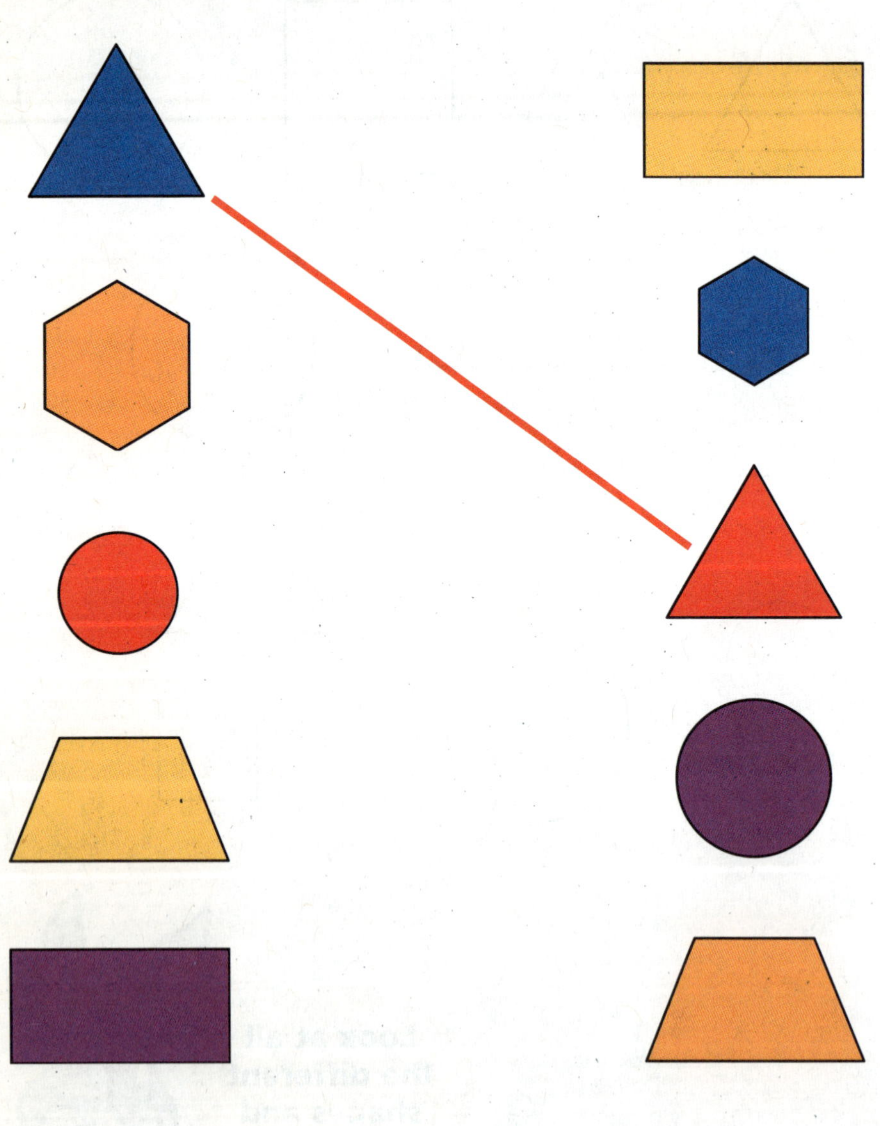

Similar objects are shaped alike.

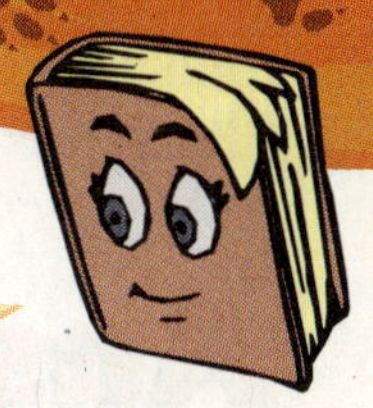

Matching Similar Shapes

Draw a line between the shapes that are alike but are different sizes. The first one has been done for you.

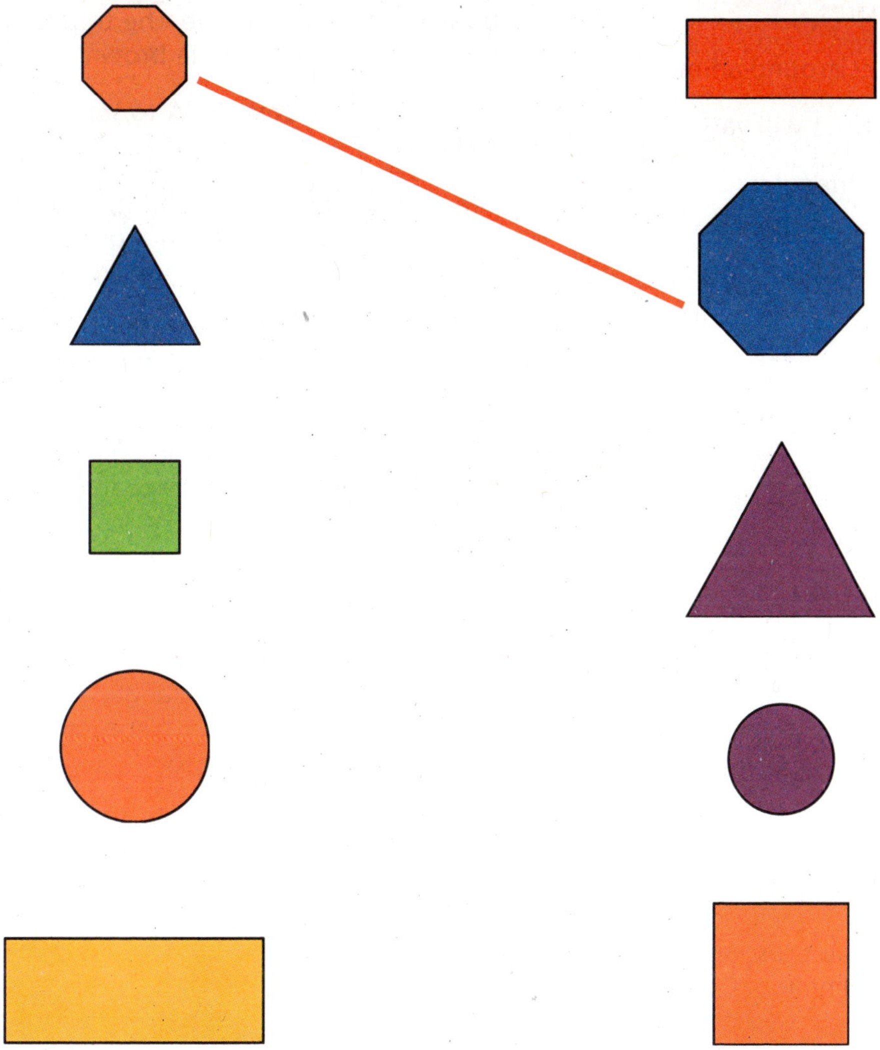

Hooray, you made it!

Have an adult help you go to **www.thelearningcompany.com/workbooks** for your certificate of completion.

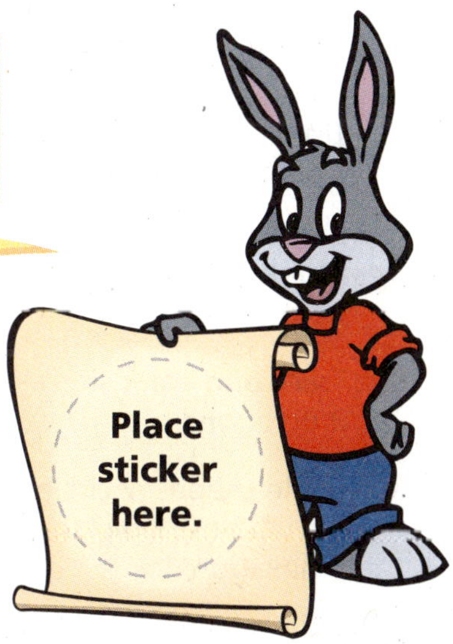

Answer Key - Find solutions for activity pages 2–31 on page 32

Page

34 Trace the square. Pictures will vary.

35 Color 7 squares. 7 squares

36 Trace and draw squares around animals.

37 Trace the triangle. Pictures will vary.

38 Draw a line through 7 triangles.

39 Color 6 green squares and 5 red triangles. 6 squares; 5 triangles

40 Trace the circle. Pictures will vary.

41 Draw an X on 9 circles. Color the picture.

42 Trace and color 9 yellow circles.

43 Trace the rectangle. Pictures will vary.

44 Color 5 rectangles. 5 rectangles

45 Trace 5 rectangles.

46 Color 8 purple circles and 6 yellow rectangles. 8 circles; 6 rectangles

47 Trace and color trapezoids.

48 Trace trapezoids. Color the trapezoid on the far right.

49 **Blue hexagons:** Kangaroo Crossing; Tigers Live Here; No Swimming; Quiet, Animals Sleeping

Red octagons: STOP; Feeding Zone; Monkeys Ahead; No Littering; Be Careful

50 Trace and color signs. 3 hexagons; 3 octagons

51 Circle shapes. 2 circles; 1 trapezoid; 3 triangles; 1 rectangle; 2 octagons; 1 hexagon

52 Color the circle red, the hexagon orange, the square green, the triangle blue, the octagon purple, the trapezoid yellow, and the rectangle brown.

53 R, E, A; write letters GREA to spell GREAT!

54 Draw square around elephant, triangle around elephant, hexagon around elephant, trapezoid around elephant.

55 Draw line from ● to *circle*, ⬡ to *hexagon*, ▲ to *triangle*, ⬢ to *octagon*, ▭ to *rectangle*.

56 Draw circles around octagon, triangle; circle, hexagon; square, trapezoid.

57 Pictures will vary.

58 Trace and color the shapes. Trace the words.

59 Color 3 squares blue, 4 triangles orange, 2 circles green, 1 trapezoid red, 5 rectangles purple.

60 Draw X on small square, big circle, small trapezoid, big triangle.

61 **Small shapes colored blue:** 2 circles, 3 triangles, 2 trapezoids, 3 squares

Large shapes colored green: 3 circles, 2 triangles, 2 trapezoids, 2 squares

62 Draw line from yellow trapezoid to orange trapezoid and purple rectangle to yellow rectangle.

63 Draw line from blue triangle to purple triangle, green square to orange square, orange circle to purple circle, yellow rectangle to red rectangle.